Clean Up City Park!

Ride Bikes, Not Cars!

We Need New Playground Equipment!

THREE PERSUASIVE LETTERS

by Cynthia Swain

Table of Contents

Focus on the Genre: Persuasive Letters 2

Letters That Made a Difference. 4

Clean Up City Park! 6

Ride Bikes, Not Cars! 12

We Need New Playground Equipment!. 16

The Writer's Craft: Persuasive Letters. 22

Glossary. 24

Make Connections
Across Texts. . . . . Inside Back Cover

Persuasive Letters

What is a persuasive letter?

A persuasive letter is a letter that tries to convince readers to believe or do something. A persuasive letter has a strong point of view about an idea or a problem. It includes facts and examples to support an opinion, and it usually suggests a solution.

What is the purpose of a persuasive letter?

People write persuasive letters to "sway," or change the minds of, their readers. They want readers to see their points of view. They may want readers to take action, too.

Who is the audience for persuasive letters?

People write persuasive letters to all kinds of people: parents, friends, citizens, business leaders, world leaders, and others. They write letters to make people understand their views. Often they want to change their audience's opinions. For example, someone might write to a leader about a law they don't agree with. The writer might want the leader to change the law.

How do you read a persuasive letter?

Keep in mind that the writer wants you to support his or her position. Ask yourself, *What is this writer's position, or opinion? Does she support it with facts and good reasons? Do I agree with her?* A good persuasive writer knows her audience. She knows what facts and reasons might change her reader's mind.

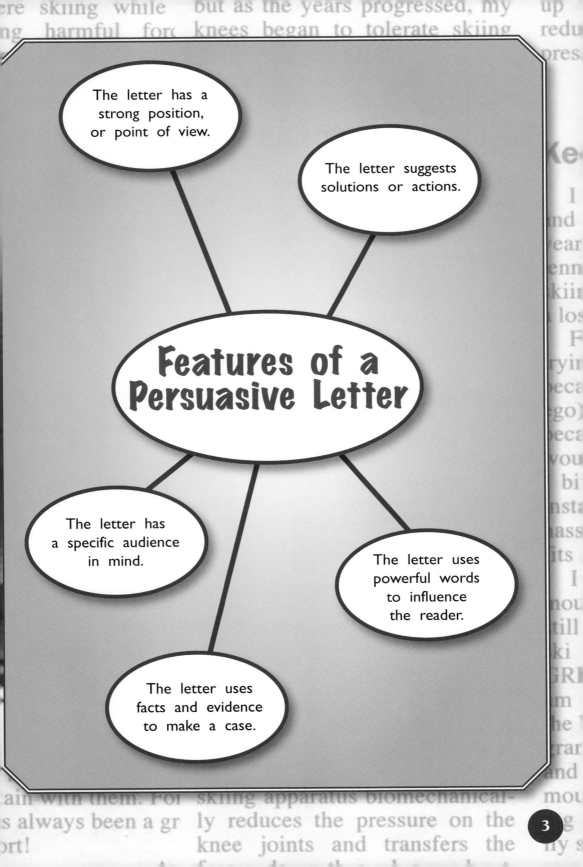

The letter has a strong position, or point of view.

The letter suggests solutions or actions.

Features of a Persuasive Letter

The letter has a specific audience in mind.

The letter uses powerful words to influence the reader.

The letter uses facts and evidence to make a case.

Letters That Made a Difference

A letter can change a person's mind. Some letters can even help change the world. People have been writing letters for centuries. Here is one example of a letter writer who made a difference.

Jane Goodall

Jane Goodall is a famous scientist. She studied chimps in Africa for many years. Then she started a group to protect animals and the environment. She has written many letters. She has written letters to people all around the world.

In one letter, Goodall wrote about animal research. She wanted people to think about whether or not to allow animal research. She said, "I am writing to you on behalf of the millions of animals each year who are subjects of laboratory experiments . . ." She asked people to hold meetings about the issue. She wanted them to learn more about what was being done to animals.

In another letter, Goodall wrote about the danger of plastic bags. She supported her position with facts. "The Environmental Protection Agency estimates that over a billion plastic bags are used each day in the United States," she said. She wanted people to stop using plastic bags. She wanted people to switch to reusable bags.

Jane Goodall is just one of many people who have used letters to make their voices heard. You can make your voice heard, too, through a letter. In this book, you will learn how.

Tools Writers Use

A Strong Ending

Persuasive texts cause readers to think, feel, or both. A strong ending is one tool writers use to meet this goal. Many persuasive texts end with an admonition, or rebuke. A rebuke says, "This is your problem, too, and we can do something about it. Doing nothing is not acceptable." Another type of persuasive ending works on the reader's emotions. These endings remind the reader of past events and ask the reader to make connections to the issue.

Clean Up City Park!

Dear Mayor,

Have you gone to City Park lately? I have. I go there every Tuesday for baseball practice. I have a game there every Saturday, too. And I can tell you that City Park is a mess. The baseball fields need repair. Trash is all over the ground. Garbage floats in the lake. You would be **heartbroken** to see the park like this. The park used to be so nice. If we don't do something, no one will go there anymore.

My dad went to City Park when he was growing up. He says that City Park used to be beautiful. His family spent every weekend in the park. People would swim. They would fish. They would have picnics. Everyone loved to go there. I wish the park were beautiful now. Now the park is a dump!

First of all, the baseball fields are dangerous. I know. I am on a team. The grass is really high. A player on my team hurt his knee. We were playing a game. The player was trying to catch a ball. He tripped on a weed. We lost the game. He couldn't play for two weeks. My dad told me, "If they don't fix those fields, you're not playing anymore." My dad is not the only parent who is upset. The parents of my teammates are worried, too. Anyone who cares about kids should be **disturbed**. This is a bad situation.

City Lake is in bad shape, too. The lake is filled with garbage. I can tell you why. There are no garbage cans. Instead, a sign tells people to take home all their garbage. But many people do not obey the sign. I know this for a fact. Last Sunday, my dad and I saw them. We were sitting on a park bench. We were watching the people. Some people did take their trash with them, but others did not! Two teenagers threw soft-drink cans into the lake. A little kid dropped his candy wrapper. A man and woman left garbage under a tree. It was a real shame!

Here is the picture I took of City Lake. Look at all the garbage!

Then my dad and I took a walk around the lake. My dad told me he used to swim in City Lake. Now nobody swims there! Dad said when he was a boy, he fished in that lake. I have never fished. I would love to fish. It would be so much fun to fish in City Lake. I bet lots of kids would like to fish there. But no one fishes there now. The water is brown. Trash is floating in the water. The trash is probably killing all the fish. Look at the picture I took of the lake. I'm sure you will feel as **disgusted** as I do.

We have to do something about City Park. We need to clean up the park. My dad told me why the city cannot take care of the park right now. The economy is bad. Many people are out of work. The people can't pay their taxes to the city. That means the city can't pay for park services. But that is no excuse. We can still take care of the park. We can find another way. Let's get volunteers to clean up the park.

Our city should have a park cleanup once a month. Volunteers could work in teams. They would pick up trash. They would cut the grass. If people knew how important this was, they would volunteer.

We could put up posters around the town. The posters would explain the cleanup effort. The posters would ask for volunteers. My baseball team would make posters. Other baseball and soccer teams would help, too. School children could make posters, too. Then parents would get involved. They will want to make the park safe and clean.

Spring is here, Mr. Mayor. Kids want to play in the park. Families want a place to have picnics. You are the leader of our city. You can do something. How will you feel if people don't have a clean, safe park? You will feel good if you help. Please think about my plan. I am ready to get into action—and so are my teammates.

Sincerely,

Jason Bolton

Understand the Letter

- Who is the writer of this letter? What does his letter tell you about him?
- What opinions does the writer express about the condition of the park? Find examples in the text.
- What do you think of the writer's plan to have volunteers clean up the park? Do you think the plan could work? Why or why not?

Analyze the Tools Writers Use: A Strong Ending

- What does this ending ask the reader to think about?
- What type of ending does this letter have? (rebuke or emotional)
- Which sentences support your answer to the second question?

Focus on Words: Words That Describe the Writer's Point of View

In this letter, the writer uses words to make the reader feel certain emotions. For example, in the first paragraph he describes the condition of the park and then says, "You would be heartbroken ..." He is telling the reader how to feel about the situation. Find other emotion words. Make a chart similar to the chart below. Define each word and think about why the writer used it.

Emotion Words

Page	Word	Dictionary Definition	Why is it an effective word choice?
7	heartbroken		
7	disturbed		
9	disgusted		

Ride Bikes, Not Cars!

Dear Citizens of Fair Hills,

Look around our town. The roads are filled with cars and vans. The air smells bad. More car accidents happen every year. I am unhappy and **distressed**. You should be, too.

Are you part of the problem? Please ask yourself these questions:

- Do I live in town?
- Do I own a car?
- Do I use my car when I could be riding a bike?

If you answered yes, then I need your help. You probably care about our town as much as I do. I know that if you understand the problem, you will want to help. So let me tell you some facts.

In 1998, our elementary school had one crossing guard. In 2008, the school had four crossing guards! Why? Because the streets are not safe anymore. The streets have  too many cars. Children cannot cross the streets alone.

In 1998, two children in our town were killed by cars. In 2008, six children were killed by cars. That is a 300% increase! That is terrible! Even one child's death is too many!

In 1998, fifteen children went to our hospital with a serious asthma attack. Last year, thirty-six children went to the hospital. Experts say that dirty air can make asthma worse. Our air has never been so dirty.

Some students at my high school measure the carbon, or soot, in our air. Their science teacher told me, "We have been measuring the carbon for five years. The carbon has gone up almost ten percent."

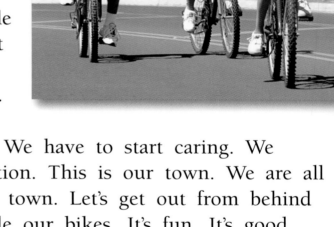

Four years ago, our town knew it had to do something. The town built bike paths. The town wanted more people to ride bikes instead of drive cars. But the number of people riding bikes has not gone up much.

Come on, people. We cannot be **apathetic** anymore. We have to start caring. We have to get into action. This is our town. We are all **responsible** for our town. Let's get out from behind the wheels. Let's ride our bikes. It's fun. It's good exercise. And it's better for our town.

Matthew Benjamin
High School Senior

Understand the Letter

- From reading his letter, what can you tell about the writer?
- Who is the writer speaking to in the letter? Does the writer know his audience personally? How can you tell?
- Why do you think the writer sent his letter to a newspaper?

Analyze the Tools Writers Use: A Strong Ending

- What does this ending ask the reader to think about?
- What type of ending does this letter have? (rebuke or emotional)
- Which sentences support your answer to the second question?

Focus on Words: Words That Describe the Writer's Point of View

Below are some strong emotion words from the letter. Make a chart similar to the chart below. Define each word and think about why the writer used it.

Emotion Words

Page	Word	Dictionary Definition	Why is it an effective word choice?
12	distressed		
14	apathetic		
14	responsible		

We Need New Playground Equipment!

Dear Principal Deets,

Do you remember when you were ten years old? Were you like me? Did you get excited when you saw a really cool playground? Do you remember how great it felt to swing up high? Did you ever close your eyes and pretend you were flying? Did you ever go to the top of the monkey bars? (And were you secretly a little afraid like I sometimes am)?

My favorite thing to do on a playground is go down the slide. I like really tall slides. I go to the top and zoom down at top speed. That is a great feeling! The best slides are metal and very smooth. You can go down them very fast.

The writer wants her reader to remember that playgrounds are fun. She describes what it feels like to be a ten-year-old kid on a playground. She would like the reader to think about playgrounds from her point of view.

16

Playgrounds are very important to ten-year-old kids. And we need them for our health, too. We spend most of our day sitting at a desk working hard. We can't move around very much. We have to hold in all our energy. Our teachers don't like us to get up and walk around. They want us to pay attention. And I understand this. If I were a teacher, I would want my students to pay attention, too. But sometimes that is very hard. Do you remember how hard it was?

Think about when you were my age. Did you ever look out your classroom window and wish it were time for recess? Well, most of the time I pay attention in class. But once in a while, I look out at the playground. And what I see is a **disappointment** to any kid who loves to play.

Our playground does not have much equipment. We have just two swings. Kids wait in a long line to use them. The monkey bars are not very big. And the slide is not very fast. The chute has too many dents in it. The seesaws give you splinters. We used to have a basketball hoop. Now the hoop is gone.

Notice that the writer describes the condition of the school's playground in great detail. She wants to support her position that the school needs new equipment.

17

Our playground is about thirty years old. My dad went to the same school. He told me the same slide was there when he was a boy. Admit it, Principal Deets: We need new playground equipment!

I know that new equipment costs money. But I think you could convince the PTA to hold a fundraiser. They got new science lab equipment last year. You told them how important the lab was. They also got new computers for the library.

Here are some things you could tell the PTA.

1. The other schools in our town have better playgrounds than we do. I took pictures of their playgrounds. I am giving you the pictures. You can show the pictures to the PTA. When they see the pictures, they will **sympathize**. They will get into action.

This writer offers photographs as evidence. She hopes that the photographs will support her position that the school needs new equipment.

18

2. Children need exercise. Most experts say children need between 60 and 90 minutes of exercise per day. One expert said exercise is "food for the brain." We don't have gym every day. We need to get some exercise at recess.

We need many kinds of exercise, too. We can't just run around. We need to build our strength. We need to build our flexibility. We need to climb on bars. We need to go on a swing or a slide. On our playground, most kids just stand around. They cannot do very much. This should be a big **concern** for the PTA.

3. We have a serious diabetes problem in our country. Children don't get enough exercise. They gain weight. When they weigh too much, they can get diabetes. The PTA could save some kids from this disease. The PTA could save some lives. They could help kids feel better about themselves, too.

The writer gives facts about why students need new playground equipment. She provides more than one argument to support her position. She knows that different people are convinced by different arguments.

This writer also appeals to her audience's emotions. She suggests that the PTA would be making the lives of children better. She assumes they would want to do this.

You should go to the PTA for these reasons. And you should go for another reason, too. You were a kid. You know how we feel. And you are our school leader. We need you. We know you care about us. We know you want what is best for us. New playground equipment will be good for us in many ways.

Sincerely,

Amanda Lewis

We need a playground like this!

REREAD THE PERSUASIVE LETTER

Understand the Letter
- Could you understand how this writer feels about her school playground?
- How did she help you understand her point of view?

Analyze the Tools Writers Use: A Strong Ending
- What does this ending ask the reader to think about?
- What type of ending does this letter have? (rebuke or emotional)
- Which sentences support your answer to the second question?

Focus on Words: Words That Describe the Writer's Point of View
Below are some strong emotion words from the letter. Make a chart similar to the chart below. Define each word and think about why the writer used it.

Emotion Words

Page	Word	Dictionary Definition	Why is it an effective word choice?
17	disappointment		
18	sympathize		
19	concern		

How does an author write a
Persuasive Letter?

Reread "We Need New Playground Equipment!" and think about what Amanda did to write this letter. How did she state her position? How did she support it effectively?

1. Choose a Problem to Write About

In a persuasive letter, the writer usually wants to talk about a problem. In this letter, the problem was the terrible condition of the school's playground equipment.

2. Identify Your Audience

The audience is the reader you are writing to. This is whom you need to convince. A writer must present facts and reasons that will convince her audience. The audience for this letter is the school principal. Amanda wrote to the principal because she knows that he can take her problem to the school PTA (Parent Teacher Association).

Problem	The school needs new playground equipment.
Audience	Mr. Deets, the school principal
Supporting Facts & Examples	• The equipment is old and in bad shape. • Every other school has better equipment. • Kids need playgrounds to get proper exercise. • Exercising can save lives and prevent diseases like diabetes.
Solution	Ask the PTA to hold a fundraiser for new playground equipment.
Ending	Appeals to the reader's emotions; asks the reader to think back to when he was a child

ere skiing while but as the years progressed, my up th
ng harmful fo knees began to tolerate skiing reduc
re to our aging n less and less. press

3. Brainstorm Facts and Examples to Support Your Position

Writers of persuasive letters support their positions with:
• facts (information that can be proven)
• concrete examples (things they have done, heard, or seen)
• supporting evidence (such as photographs)

4. Provide a Solution to the Problem and a Strong Ending

A writer may provide one or more solutions. In this letter, Amanda gave many reasons why the school should have new playground equipment. Amanda gave supporting facts and examples to convince the principal.

GLOSSARY

apathetic (a-puh-THEH-tik) uninterested (page 14)

concern (kun-SERN) worry (page 19)

disappointment (dis-uh-POINT-ment) regret (page 17)

disgusted (dih-SKUS-ted) sickened (page 9)

distressed (dih-STREST) upset (page 12)

disturbed (dih-STERBD) troubled (page 7)

heartbroken (HART-broh-ken) saddened; without hope (page 7)

responsible (rih-SPAHN-suh-bul) in charge (page 14)

sympathize (SIM-puh-thize) to have the same feeling or belief as someone else (page 18)